YOUR KNOWLEDGE HAS VALUE

- We will publish your bachelor's and master's thesis, essays and papers

- Your own eBook and book - sold worldwide in all relevant shops

- Earn money with each sale

Upload your text at www.GRIN.com
and publish for free

Bibliographic information published by the German National Library:

The German National Library lists this publication in the National Bibliography; detailed bibliographic data are available on the Internet at http://dnb.dnb.de .

Imprint:

Copyright © 2014 GRIN Verlag, Open Publishing GmbH
Print and binding: Books on Demand GmbH, Norderstedt Germany
ISBN: 9783668444218

This book at GRIN:

http://www.grin.com/en/e-book/358125/delaunay-tetrahedralization-and-its-dual-voronoi-diagrams

Maria Vineeta

Delaunay Tetrahedralization and its dual Voronoi Diagrams

GRIN Publishing

GRIN - Your knowledge has value

Since its foundation in 1998, GRIN has specialized in publishing academic texts by students, college teachers and other academics as e-book and printed book. The website www.grin.com is an ideal platform for presenting term papers, final papers, scientific essays, dissertations and specialist books.

Visit us on the internet:

http://www.grin.com/

http://www.facebook.com/grincom

http://www.twitter.com/grin_com

Abstract

The Delaunay tetrahedralization is one of the most popular and common method used for solving problems related to meshes. It is either used for generating a mesh or for breaking it up, as Voronoi diagrams, dual of the DT is a commonly used process for that. The main task of this project is to implement a robust Delaunay Tetrahedralization structure, with a set of points generated from sampling a given 3D Mesh.

Points within the volume of the mesh can be obtained by several methods. We present two such methods and discuss the result obtained. These points serve as vertices for the tetrahedrons that are a part of the combinatorial structure DT.

3D Delaunay Tetrahedralization(DT) is not as optimal as 2D Delaunay triangulations. Implementing them gives rise to several degeneracies, which are quite difficult to handle. In this project, we have implemented a simple Incremental Insertion Algorithm based on the paper presented by Ledoux(2007), inorder to construct the DT structure. Correctness of the structure is given utmost importance rather than its speed.

Acknowledgements

I would like to thank my programme co-ordinator Jon Macey for his assistance. I would also like to thank Dr. Xiaosong Yang for rendering his valuable time to assist me with my project. I would also like to thank Mathieu Sanchez for his guidance in this project and for allowing me to use his SDF library in my project.

Contents

Chapter 1

Introduction

Meshes composed of triangles or tetrahedra are used in various applications like terrain databases, Geographical Information Systems, but most demandingly, in Mesh Generation and obtaining partial differential solution using Finite Element Method. There have been several algorithms that explains how to generate the triangles or tetrahedra given a set of points. Although they are used for various applications, the central focus of this thesis is computing Tetrahedrons within a 3D Mesh and thereafter obtain its dual, the Voronoi diagram, using Delaunay Tetrahedralization for the purpose of Fracturing a 3D Mesh.

Fracturing of objects(Destruction) is becoming a key aspect in any major visual effects pipeline. A typical destruction pipeline's basic step involves preparing the 3d object for fracture. Although, there are several ways to prepare the 3D object, the most common and widely used is shattering using Voronoi diagrams(VD). The VD can be computed directly given a set of points using several algorithms. Pipelines that already exist are either based on Rigid Body Simulations or on a new solution, Finite Element Analysis(FEA) . The majority of the algorithms used in these pipelines do not compute the VD directly as additional computations on intermediate voronoi vertices are performed which greatly reduces the speed of the algorithm. Instead the Voronoi Diagram needed is extracted from its dual, the Delaunay triangulation directly without the need for additional computations and hence has the advantage of speeding up algorithms.

The process of breaking a 3d Mesh into triangles is called Triangulation. This can be achieved by a method called Delaunay Triangulation(DT). DT for a set of points can be obtained by checking the empty circle criterion for any triangle in DT(P). The triangle is said to be Delaunay only if the circumcircle of every triangle is empty, i.e has no other points or vertices. This can be extended to three and higher dimension, when circumsphere is considered. In three dimensions the primitives are no longer triangles, but tetrahedra, hence the process is termed Tetrahedralization. A circumsphere check is considered here to check if the Tetrahedron is Delaunay.

This thesis focuses specifically on the creation of Tetrahedrons using Delaunay Tetrahedralization and thus extracting its dual Voronoi Diagram.

In Chapter 2, we present several work done related to Delaunay Tetrahedralization. We further extend the discussion to its applications.

In Chapter 3, we present the main idea behind generation of points inside the Mesh using two different methods Ray Casting and SDF.

In Chapter 4, the construction of Delaunay Tetrahedrons and the various algorithms used for generating it are discussed. The main algorithm used in this project is explained in the succeeding sub-chapters. The degeneracies that will occur for the algorithm chosen are also discussed.

In Chapter 5, the implementation details of the algorithm are explained. The problems occured while implementing them and the limitations of the algorithm are presented.

In Chapter 6, we evaluate the work done. The drawbacks and advantages of the algorithm implemented are portrayed. Furthermore, its use in recent scenario and future work are briefly discussed.

Chapter 2

Related work

Delaunay triangulation is one of the most popular and most often used methods in problems mainly related to computational geometry. It was discovered in 1934 by the French mathematician Boris Nikolaevich Delone or Delaunay. Many of the Delaunay properties were intensively studied only in 2D for many years. It was extensively researched in the engineering community since the mid – 1980s. For instance, Frey in 1987 presented a solution for eliminating badly shaped triangles from their triangulation by inserting a new vertex at their circumcenters . Similarly Weatherill (1992) gives an alternate solution by inserting vertices at their centroids. These ideas were very helpful when problems related to Mesh generation started evolving in the early 1990s.

Delaunay Triangulations have been constructed in two and three dimensions using several interesting algorithms : sweep- plane, divide-and-conquer and incremental insertion. All these algorithms yields an optimal solution in two dimensions. In 1985, Guibas and Stolfi (1985) proposed a Divide and Conquer algorithm which achieves the optimal bound of O(n log n). Later, Steve Fortune (1987) proposed a Sweepline algorithm for Voronoi diagrams which also achieves this bound. However, when it comes to three-dimensions, things get a bit more complicated. Cignoni et.al(1998) manages to compute DeWall algorithm for constructing the DT in any dimensions, based on the divide-and-conquer algorithm (Fortune 1987). But, Shewchuck(1997) suggests using plan-sweep paradigm for the construction of constrained DT as it is sub-optimal when compared to the former. Unfortunately, these algorithms requires significant programming complexity. Hence, incremental insertion is preferred over the two as it is quite simple to implement and less-error prone.

Incremental insertion can be implemented using two algorithms : Bowyer-Watson Algorithm (1981) and flip-based Algorithm. Flip based algorithm is chosen over Bowyer-Watson as the latter is more error-prone because of the creation of holes, which occur when deleting a conflicting Tetrahedra that does not satisfy the Delaunay criterion. Lawson (1977) developed the first flip-based algorithm in two dimensions. While using the same concept of Lawson for higher dimensions, Joe (1989)proves that the algorithm fails when the union of the two tetrahedra is concave. However, Joe (1991) solves this problem and proves that flip based algorithm works for higher dimensions as well.

In recent years, several Mesh Generators namely Tetgen and Netgen have emerged. Tetgen is a quality tetrahedral Mesh Generator developed by HangSi (2004). It is designed in C++ and is used for constructing Delaunay tetrahedralization, voronoi diagram and convex hull for three-dimensional point sets. Tetgen initially was implemented using a randomized incremental flip-based algorithm of Edelsbrunner and Shah(1996). The algorithm is fast and memory efficient. The latest version of Tetgen as updated on 2009, uses a new implementation of the Bowyer-Watson Algorithm for Delaunay Tetrahedralization. Hang Si, proves that it is faster than incremental flip based algorithm.

Similarly, Netgen is an automatic mesh generation tool in two and three dimension developed by Joachim Schoberl(1994). It uses Constructive Solid Geometry(CSG) as its domain input format for generating tetrahedral meshes in 3D.

Computation Geometry Algorithms Library(CGAL) is an open source library offers data structures and algorithms for creating Triangulations in 2D and 3D. CGAL also uses incremental insertion algorithm, but uses Bowyer-Watson instead of flipping. For locating a point in the structure, it employs Delaunay hierarchy (Devillers 2002).

Chapter 3

Mesh Sampling

A Delaunay tetrahedralization, takes as input a set of points to construct the DT structure. These points are obtained by sampling a given 3D Mesh.

There are several algorithms to obtain points on the surface of a mesh. The easiest being, generating random points along the triangles of a polygonal mesh using Barycentric co-ordinates. But, for certain applications like Fracturing, points are needed in positions along the volume of the source mesh. Inorder to place samples, not just on the surface but also in the volume enclosed by a mesh, we present two methods.

3.1 Ray Intersection

Ray intersection is a very straightforward way of obtaining points inside the volume of a mesh. To begin with, the bounding box of the given mesh is calculated. And then, several random points are generated on the surface of this bounding box. The method we used is the same as obtaining sample points on a triangle using Barycentric co-ordinates as depicted in Figure 3.11(Jose 2011). The bounding box is triangulated and random points are then obtained on the triangles of the bounding box.

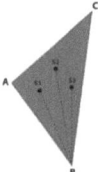

Figure 3.11 Random points on a triangle

We start with two variables u and v with random values between 0 and 1 such that $u + v <= 1$. The resulting point is obtained by the weighted sum of the triangle vertices, such as,

$$S_i = u * A + v * B + w * C \qquad \text{where,}$$

$$w = 1 - (u + v)$$

After generating random points on the bounding box, we shoot rays iteratively joining two random points on opposite faces of the bounding box. Each ray will intersect the geometry in a number of segments indicated by red dashed lines in Figure 3.12. Every segment is defined by an entry and an exit point. The pros of this approach is that it fits the mesh perfectly and precisely obtain the intersection points of the ray on the mesh . The cons of using this approach is that, it may be a bit slow and the distribution is far from ideal for few samples-although it tends to converge decently when the number of requested samples increases. This can be managed by increasing the density of rays instead of the number of samples generated per segment of the ray. The number of samples on a segment depends on a 'linear density factor'. It is calculated as length of segment * density, where density depends on the number of samples requested and the volume of the bounding box (Jose 2011).

Figure 3.12 Ray intersection

3.2 Signed Distance Field

A distance field function provides the shortest distance to an object from an arbitrary point in space. The sign of the function determines if the point is inside or outside the object. This technique can be used to generate random points within the mesh. As done in the previous method, random points are generated within the bounding box using a simple random function.

Distance field function computes the shortest distance of every point to the mesh, by comparing the distance from the point to each triangle. The sign of the function is computed by a scanning method. A grid is scanned starting from a corner that is definitely outside the object and if a cell is crossed by the surface, the sign is changed. However, this solution works best only for a discrete function. For a continuous function, the sign can be computed using the sign of the dot product between the surface normal at the closest point and the vector from P to the closest point.

The downside in using SDF is that, computing the signed distance field on larger meshes can become time consuming. Computing the distance to every single polygon of the mesh is largely inefficient and does not take advantage of the spatial coherence. Optimization can be done by using spatial partitioning, hierarchy trees and square distances.

Chapter 4

Constructing DT

There are several paradigms in computational geometry for computing the DT in two and three dimensions. However, constructing a DT in three dimensions is quite complicated. In this thesis we have used Incremental insertion algorithm, as this has the complexity $O(n^2)$ which is worst case-optimal. With this algorithm, every point is inserted into the DT one at a time. The tetrahedra containing the newly added point is partitioned and new tetrahedrons are created thus updating the DT structure.

By inserting each point one at a time, we observe that only the Delaunay tetrahedra local to the point is altered and not the entire structure. Whereas in the other two paradigm, divide-and-conquer and sweep plane, the entire structure is built in a single operation. Inserting a new vertex would result in computing the whole structure again. Hence, incremental insertion is mandatory when a dynamic spatial model is built . The insertion of a single point can be achieved with two incremental insertion algorithms

1) the Bowyer-Watson algorithm and
2) flip-based algorithm.

The idea behind Bowyer-Watson(1981) is very simple. Tetrahedrons that does not satisfy the Delaunay criterion when a point is inserted, are deleted. However, this method is prone to errors as it forms a 'gap' or 'hole' when the tetrahedrons are deleted and affects the overall topological structure as well. Hence, flip based algorithm is preferred over the former. The rest of this chapter we discuss the Incremental Flip-based algorithm.

4.1 Initialisation

Let S be the point set. We first start with a single boundary tetrahedron, constructed in such a way that it encompasses the whole set of points, S. The initial tetrahedron constructed should be several times larger than the range of S as depicted in Figure 4.11 which illustrates a two-dimensional example. This serves as the initial structure for the construction of DT(S), then the points are inserted one by one and the structure is updated. This approach always ensures that the point to be inserted is always within an existing tetrahedron, which avoids unnecessary operations of dealing with points outside the boundary. The main downside is that, additional tetrahedrons than needed are constructed. The tetrahedron that has atleast one boundary point as vertex has to be eliminated in the end.

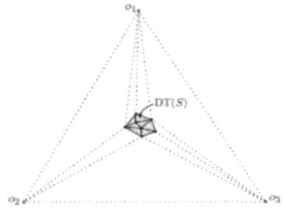

Figure 4.11 Set of points (s) bounded by the triangle O_1, O_2 and O_3.

4.2 Predicates

The incremental insertion algorithm makes its important decisions based on the result of two main geometric tests : (Ledoux)

- *Orient* determines if a point P is above, below or on a plane defined by three points A, B and C.
- *InSphere* determines if a point P is inside or outside or on a sphere determined by four points A,B,C and D.

These two can be obtained as shown by the computation of the determinant of a matrix. These two predicates can also be implemented by translating all the points by P, and then computing the determinant as applying an identical translation will not affect the result. Thus it can be reduced to 3x3 and 4x4 matrices.

$$Orient(A, B, C, P) = \begin{vmatrix} A_x & A_y & A_z & 1 \\ B_x & B_y & B_z & 1 \\ C_x & C_y & C_z & 1 \\ P_x & P_y & P_z & 1 \end{vmatrix}$$

$$= \begin{vmatrix} A_x - P_x & A_y - P_y & A_z - P_z \\ B_x - P_x & B_y - P_y & B_z - P_z \\ C_x - P_x & C_y - P_y & C_z - P_z \end{vmatrix}$$

$$InSphere(A, B, C, D, P) = \begin{vmatrix} A_x & A_y & A_z & (A_x^2 + A_y^2 + A_z^2) & 1 \\ B_x & B_y & B_z & (B_x^2 + B_y^2 + B_z^2) & 1 \\ C_x & C_y & C_z & (C_x^2 + C_y^2 + C_z^2) & 1 \\ D_x & D_y & D_z & (D_x^2 + D_y^2 + D_z^2) & 1 \\ P_x & P_y & P_z & (P_x^2 + P_y^2 + P_z^2) & 1 \end{vmatrix}$$

$$= \begin{vmatrix} A_x - P_x & A_y - P_y & A_z - P_z & (A_x - P_x)^2 + (A_y - P_y)^2 + (A_z - P_z)^2 \\ B_x - P_x & B_y - P_y & B_z - P_z & (B_x - P_x)^2 + (B_y - P_y)^2 + (B_z - P_z)^2 \\ C_x - P_x & C_y - P_y & C_z - P_z & (C_x - P_x)^2 + (C_y - P_y)^2 + (C_z - P_z)^2 \\ D_x - P_x & D_y - P_y & D_z - P_z & (D_x - P_x)^2 + (D_y - P_y)^2 + (D_z - P_z)^2 \end{vmatrix}$$

4.2.1 Robustness

Using floating point arithmetic for these matrices, offers only an approximation number, hence the consequence of using it should be well understood. The combinatorial structure like DT, whose construction is based only on these two predicates, a slightly different value could affect the whole structure. Hence, the use of exact arithmetic is essential. The value of the determinant is not of utmost importance but rather the sign of the determinant is. Also, we should be able to detect if it the value of the determinant is exactly zero. For instance, five cospherical points by Insphere can be considered not cospherical because the result of the determinant is not exactly 0 (Ledoux 2007).

Schewchuck(1997) presents a simple solution for the robustness problem. This is very important for the correctness of the DT as it is tightly linked with the special cases we will have to deal with. The major obstacle in using exact arithmetic is that it reduces the speed of computation badly. Hence, Schewchuck(1997) in his paper has used exact arithmetic only for determining the sign thus working as a filter that will activate the function only when needed. He states that "These predicates cost a little more than ordinary non-robust predicates, but never sacrifice correctness for speed".

4.3 Point Location

Given a *DT* structure of *T* Tetrahedrons constructed with the points in *S*, we need to determine which Tetrahedron the point to be inserted is in. The task of locating a point and navigating through the triangulations has been central problem to a number of computational geometry applications. There are several algorithms for point location in triangulations. Many of them are optimal, but they are quite complex to implement and use extra storage during pre-processing for creating additional data structure. Hence, practitioners prefer sub-optimal algorithms that avoids such problems are are quite easy to implement.

4.3.1 Walking

Green and Sibson (1977) presented an algorithm referred to as "Walking" that does not require any additional storage and pre-processing. This algorithm was considered to provide fast practical solution for constructing a dynamic structure, based on experimental results by Devillers et al.(2002) and Mucke et al (1999). Later Guibas and Stolfi (1985) provided the pseudo-code for the algorithm presented by Green and Sibson (1977). In three and higher dimensions the algorithm is a bit more intricate. We will explain the algorithm in detail specifically for three dimension.

Given a vertex q of $T(u,v,w,q)$ and a query point p, the initial step of the algorithm is, finding the tetrahedron, adjacent to T and incident to q as shown in Figure 4.31. The adjacent tetrahedron is chosen such that the point q and p are on either side of the plane defined by u,v and w. This is achieved by performing two orientation test (predicate) involving the point q and p. The adjacent Tetrahedron found becomes T, and the traversing continues until no such adjacent tetrahedron is found. When such a situation arises, it is concluded that T has the point. Making the algorithm robust is not necessary as it is not affected by the degenerate cases.

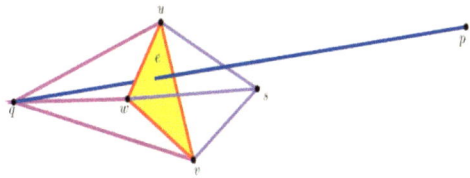

Figure 4.31 Walking in 3D

4.4 Incremental flip based Algorithm

An alternative to Bowyer-Watson algorithm is to use bistellar flips to alter the tetrahedrons in the vicinity of P, that does not satisfy the Delaunay criterion. A bistellar flip is a local topological operation that modifies the configuration of adjacent triangles in a triangulation, tetrahedron in case of 3D. Although by using this algorithm, the computation speed is reduced due to flippability tests and more tetrahedron than needed are created, it is advantageous, as its simple to implement and less error-prone since the adjacency relationships in a DT is encapsulated in the flip operations.

4.4.1 Two Dimension

The flip based algorithm was first constructed by Lawson (1977) only for two-dimensional triangulations. He states that, flipping edges of an arbitrary triangulations of a set of points S, can transform this triangulation into any other triangulation of S, including the Delaunay triangulation. This algorithm runs with $O(n^2)$ complexity, since there exists $O(n)$ triangles that must be tested against each other. This can be improved to $O(nlogn)$, by using incremental insertion algorithm based on edge flipping. The process of inserting a single point P, by this method is illustrated in Figure 4.41. To begin with, the triangle containing the query point is determined. This triangle is split into three new triangles, incident to P. Then, each new triangle is tested against its opposite neighbour, according to the Delaunay criterion. If the triangle does not satisfy that criteria, the edge shared by the triangle with its neighbour, is flipped, and these two new triangles are further tested later. This process ends only when every triangle, that has P as one of its vertices satisfies the Delaunay criterion.

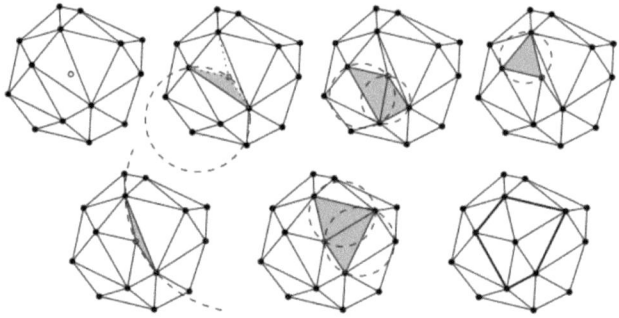

Figure 4.41 Two dimensional step-by-step implementation of flip based algorithm

4.4.2 Three dimension

The flip based algorithm usually extends to higher dimensions as well. But, Lawson's algorithm (1977) fails for higher dimensions. Joe (1989) proves that it is not possible for a non-locally Delaunay facet to flip when the union of two tetrahedral that shares that common facet is concave. Later, Joe(1991) invented a solution to this problem, where he claims that atleast one sequence of flips elsewhere will always be possible when constructing the DT, even when non-Delaunay facets impossible to flip occur. His research formed the basis for the construction of the Delaunay tetrahedralization.

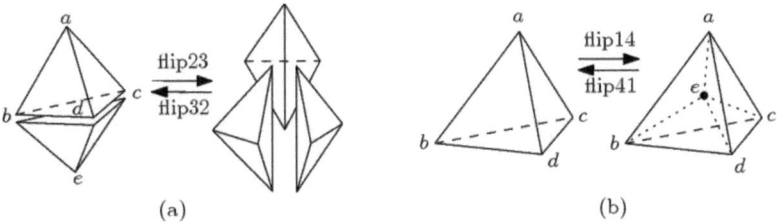

Figure 4.42 Bistellar flips in 3D

Consider a set $S = \{a, b, c, d, e\}$ of points in R^3, and its initial boundary tetrahedron, which becomes the convex hull of S, denoted conv(S). Two possible configurations exist as depicted in Figure 4.42(Ledoux 2007).

- The five points of S lie on the boundary of conv(S); see Figure 4.42(a). According to Lawson(1986) there are exactly two ways to tetrahedralize such a polyhedron:either with two or three tetrahedra. In the first case, the two tetrahedral share a triangulated face bcd, and in the latter case, the two tetrahedral all have a common edge ae.
- One point e of S does not lie on the boundary of conv(S), thus conv($\underline{S}$) forms a tetrahedron; see Figure 4.42(b). The only way to tetrahedralize S is with four tetrahedral all incident to e.

Depending on these two configurations, Ledoux states that four types of flips are possible.

- *Flip23* occurs when S is considered to be in the first configuration. As the name suggests, this operation transforms a tetrahedralization of two tetrahedra into another one with three tetrahedra. From Figure 4.42(a) if the triangular face bcd does not satisfy the Delaunay criterion locally, then a flip23 will occur, creating three new tetrahedra.
- *Flip32* is the inverse of *Flip23*.
- *Flip 14* happens when a point is inserted into the tetrahedralization. The point becomes a vertex when Flip14 occurs splitting the tetrahedron that contains the point into four new tetrahedra, all incident to that point.
- *Flip41* is the inverse of *Flip14* that deletes a vertex and transforms four tetrahedra into one.

Bistellar flips do not always apply to adjacent tetrahedral[20] (Joe, 1989). Unlike in two dimensions, these flips are performed only if certain geometric conditions are satisfied. For instance ,a flip23 is possible on two tetrahedra that are adjacent to each other, only if the union of the two tetrahedra abcd and bcde is a convex polyhedron, implying that the line ae passes through the common triangular face bcd. If not, then a flip32 might be possible, only if it has a third tetrahedron adjacent to both abcd and bcde.

Unlike in two dimensions, the flips are implemented based on certain geometric conditions depending on T and T_a. Different cases arise when we view the tetrahedron T_a from the point p. In three dimensions, three types of tetrahedra are possible, when viewed from a fixed point.

Case 1 : Only one facet of T_a is visible. This is possible when the edge joining the two apexes of T and Ta passes through the interior of their common facet. Therefore, the union of the two tetrahedra is a convex polyhedron. When such a case occurs, flip23 is performed.(Figure 4.43)

Case 2 : When two faces of Ta are visible. The edge joining the two apexes of T and Ta does not pass through the common facet, implies that the union of the two tetrahedron are concave. In such a case, if a third tetrahedron pabd occurs as shown in Figure 4.43 , then a flip32 is possible. If the third tetrahedron doesn't exist, then no flip is performed.

When three facets are visible, no flip is performed and the next tetrahedron in the stack is processed.

The algorithm to implement the Incremental flip based method handling all the cases is described in Section 5.2

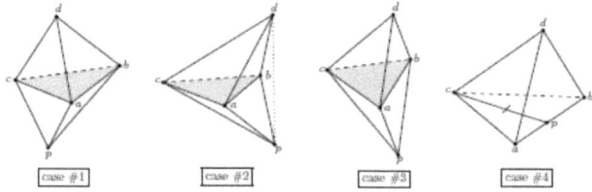

Figure 4.43 Different cases that occur while flipping

4.4.3 Degeneracies

While constructing the DT in three dimensions, several degeneracies tend to occur. For instance when the edge connecting the two apexes of T and T_a gives unexpected results. The degeneracies that occur and the solution to handle it are presented in case3 and case4 as follows :

Case 3 : if the line segment intersects an edge directly instead of the face, then the vertices p,a,d and b are coplanar thus resulting in a flat tetrahedron. A flip44 is possible only if the two tetrahedra contains two more tetrahedra adjacent to them such that, all the four tetrahedral are in config44 as shown in Figure 4.43

Case 4 : As shown in Figure 4.43, the point might be inserted directly onto an edge of a tetrahedron, which has resulted in this situation. To solve this issue, it is enough if a flip23 is performed on T and Ta. This will definitely created another flat tetrahedron, but it was proven that the flat tetrahedron created would be deleted in another flip.

Other degeneracies occur depending on the location of the point to be inserted in the existing tetrahedralized structure. Some of the degenerate cases that occur when the point is inserted,

- directly on the circumsphere of another tetrahedron in T.

- No flip is performed.
- exactly on the vertex of another Tetrahedron in T.
  - the distance of the point p to each vertex of the tetrahedron T returned by WALK is tested against a tolerance value. If the distance is found smaller than the tolerance, p is not inserted at all.
- directly on a face of a Tetrahedron in T.
  - No special treatment is required as the flat tetrahedron that results after flip14 will be deleted when tested against its neighbour in another flip.

4.4.4 Time Complexity

The running time for implementing incremental insertion algorithm for a set S of n points is $O(n^2)$ in worst case. It was later proved that this can be reduced to $O(n \log n)$ if the n points were distributed uniformly (Edelsbrunner and Shah 1996). Also notice that, every flip deletes only one-non Delaunay tetrahedron and replaces few new ones. For instance, flip14, removes only one tetrahedron and replaces four new tetrahedra. Also, flip23, removes one conflicting tetrahedron that does not satisfy the Delaunay criterion and replaces it by three new tetrahedral incident to point p. Similarly flip32, removes a conflicting tetrahedron and replaces it by two new ones, incident to p. Also notice that, once a conflicting tetrahedron is removed after a flip, it is not re-introduced into the Tetrahedralization T. Hence, it can be concluded that if there are n tetrahedra conflicting with point p, then exactly n flips are needed to construct the DT.

4.5 Duality between DT and VD

It is quite easy to construct the Voronoi diagram from the DT structure as its the dual of the latter. Each element of the DT corresponds exactly to one and only one other element of the Voronoi structure defined as follows :

Vertex : The Voronoi vertex is quite easily obtained from the DT, as it is the center of the sphere circumscribed to its dual Tetrahedron. Thus the Delaunay vertex, p becomes a Voronoi cell as shown in Figure 4.51(a).

Face : a Delaunay edge is dual to a Voronoi face(Figure 4.51(b)). It is obtained by all the vertices dual to the tetrahedra incident to a Delaunay edge. In simple words, obtain all voronoi vertices of the tetrahedra around the Delaunay edge.

Edge : a Voronoi edge is formed by two voronoi vertices if and only if their dual tetrahedra are adjacent to each other (Figure 4.51(c)).

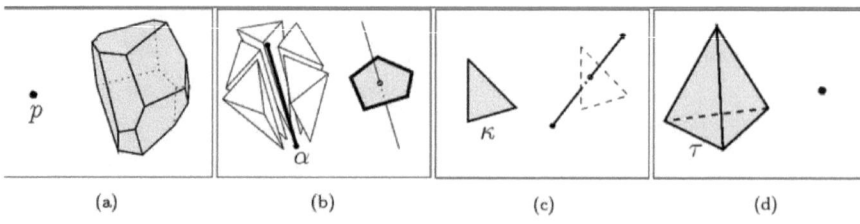

Figure 4.51 Duality between VD and DT elements in 3D

Polyhedron : A Delaunay vertex p becomes a Voronoi cell as shown in Figure 4.51(d). It is constructed by all the Voronoi vertices dual to the tetrahedral, incident to the Delaunay vertex p.

For the VD, degeneracies tend to occur depending on the distribution of points. Since, the construction of the VD is dependant on DT, much care is taken to ensure the correctness of DT.

Chapter 5

Implementation

The Delaunay tetrahedralization have been developed in C++ using the NGL library. The initial part of the project, obtaining volume samples was implemented based on the idea given by Jose(2011) in his blog. The sample points are obtained using two methods Ray Intersections and SDF. Points generated using Signed distance field relies on the SDF library developed by Sanchez (2009).

The UI for generating points is designed in such a way, points can be generated either on the surface of the mesh or within the mesh depending on user request. Surface point generation and Ray intersection method both use the principle of Barycentric-cordinates to generate random points within a triangle. A class called *MeshSampler* is implemented to handle the two methods used for generation of points. Figure 5.1 illustrates the implementation of this technique and is tested with different meshes. The red points indicates the required point set generated. The green dots are the surface points on the Bounding box from which rays are generated as shown in Figure 5.1. The ray intersection with the mesh is determined, and the segment within the mesh interpolated to obtain the points within the mesh.

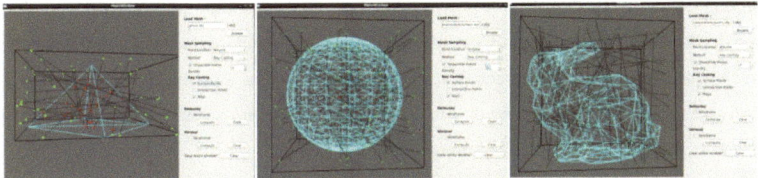

Figure 5.1 Mesh Sampling using Ray intersections

Similarly, samples are obtained using SDF library. This is depicted in Figure 5.2.

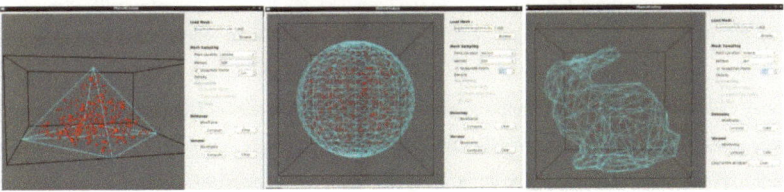

Figure 5.2 Mesh sampling using SDF

Though visually the difference is not evident, while implementing both the algorithms, it was quite obvious, the computational speed of Ray marching was very slow when compared to SDF. Though it has the advantage of not constructing additional vertices outside the mesh, unlike SDF, it didn't work very well when the density of points was increased. Another downside in using ray intersection is that, with a complicated concave mesh and for a density of 1000 as shown in Figure 5.3, the ray intersection algorithm produces erroneous results and generates some points outside the mesh boundary(see Figure 5.3(a)) On the other hand, SDF works perfectly well for any kind of Mesh.(see Figure 5.3(b)).

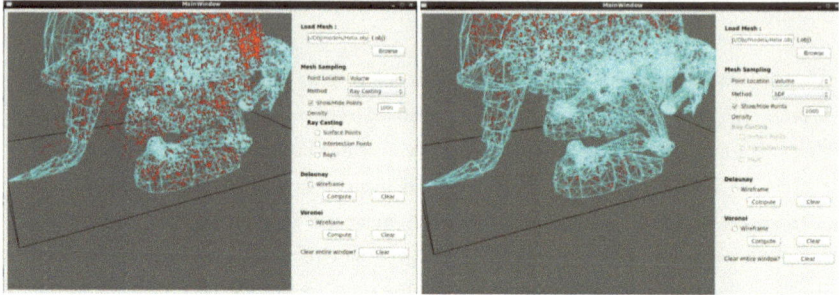

Figure 5.3 (a) Points sampled using Ray intersections (b) Points sampled using SDF

Having constructed the point set S, the DT can be constructed by implementing Incremental insertion algorithm. The algorithm implemented in this thesis is based on the paper presented by Ledoux. Ledoux has presented a clear and complete explanation on how Voronoi diagrams and its dual Delaunay tetrahedrons can be computed. Degenerate cases that occur while constructing the DT and the solution on how to handle it is also presented by him. The algorithm implemented is explained in Section 5.1. The data structure used to store DT is quite important, and a simple tetrahedron-based data structure is used in the implementation of the algorithm. This structure is advantageous as it is quite fast and space efficient. The class *Tetrahedron* uses this data structure, containing four of its vertices and a pointer to its four adjacent tetrahedra.

5.1 Algorithm : InsertOnePoint(*T*,*p*)

To begin with, the first point *p* is inserted into the boundary tetrahedron that acts as the conv(*S*). This point splits the boundary tetrahedron into four new tetrahedra with *flip14*. These four tetrahedra created are inserted into a stack. This stack contains all the tetrahedra yet to be checked against the Delaunay criterion. As the algorithm progresses all the new tetrahedra created after a flip are inserted into this stack. The algorithm stops when the stack becomes empty, meaning that all the tetrahedra incident to point P are Delaunay. The algorithm is as follows (Ledoux 2007).

Input   : A DT(*S*) *T* in R^3 and a new point p to be inserted.

Output : A tetrahedralization, *T U {p}* where all tetrahedral incident to *p* are Delaunay.

  T = WALK(tetrahedra containing P).

17

do *flip14*, splitting T into four new tetrahedra incident to *p*.

Push the four new tetrahedra on a stack (*TS*)

while *TS* non-empty **do**

    $T = \{p,a,b,c\}$ ← pop from stack

    $T^a = \{a,b,c,d\}$ ← get the tetrahedron adjacent of T having abc facet

    if (d is inside circumsphere of *T*) **then**

        FLIP(T, T_a)

    endif

end while

5.2 Algorithm : FLIP(T, T_a)

As presented by Ledoux(2007).

Input : Two adjacent tetrahedra T and T_a.

if case1 **then**

    flip23(T, T_a)

    push tetrahedra *pabd,pbcd and pacd* on stack

else if case2 AND third tetrahedron *pdab* exists **then**

    flip32($T, T_a, pdab$)

    push *pacd* and *pbcd* on stack

else if case3 AND T and T_a are in config44 with T_b and T_c **then**

    flip44(T, T_a, T_b, T_c)

    push on stack the four tetrahedral created

else if case4 **then**

    flip23(T, T_a)

    push tetrahedra *pabd, pbcd and pacd* on stack

end if

5.3 Robustness

Having implemented the above algorithm, didn't yield the correct structure. Several tetrahedrons were overlapping each other. Also, certain points were not included in the final DT structure constructed(see Figure 5.31). It was quite frustrating during the development of this process, as the source of the problem was not known for a long time. Tweaking the code to fix a particular problem resulted in another problem somewhere else. The program constantly kept crashing if the number of points were increased. The problem was later identified as the use of floating point arithmetic, which

18

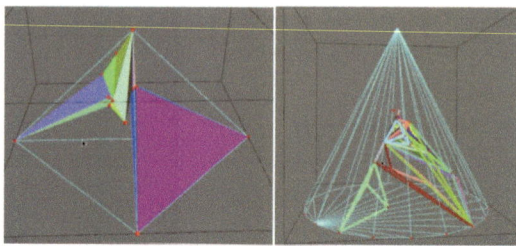

Figure 5.31 Error due to floating-point arithmetic

yields only an approximation to real numbers. The immediate fix thought was the use of a tolerance value, but it didn't yield satisfactory results for a complicated structure like DT. As the incremental insertion algorithm makes the important decision of which flips to apply, depending on the two geometric predicates, *Orient* and *InSphere* discussed in Section 4.2., it is important that these two predicates yield the exact results.

Schewchuck (1997) presented a solution for this issue. It is concluded that exact arithmetic is very important while constructing the DT or the whole structure would be affected. The downside to this is that the implementation speed is greatly affected. However, Schewchuck (1997) presents an adaptive technique, where the exact arithmetic was used only to determine the sign of the determinant and not its value, thus saving on the computational speed.

5.4 Results

A step by step implementation of the algorithm, where the points are inserted into the tetrahedron one at a time is as shown in Figure 5.41. The image numbered 6 in the Figure is the final DT structure obtained after deleting the tetrahedrons containing the initial big tetrahedron.

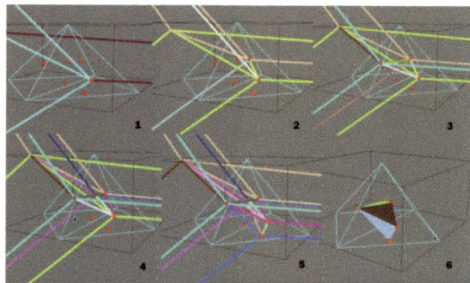

Figure 5.41 Step by step implementation of the insertion algorithm

It is noted that the spatial distribution of points affects the construction of the DT. When points generated using Ray intersection are used, the algorithm tends to crash some times,especially when the density of points is higher. However, when points obtained using SDF are used, the DT is constructed perfectly. Figure 5.42 shows the DT obtained using SDF for a cube mesh

Figure 5.42 DT of a cube and its wireframe , with density of points = 100

As the density of points increases, the processing speed gets affected. But, since our focus was to obtain an accurate terahedralization structure, this was quite acceptable. However, when a user interface was provided, it is designed in such a way that the density of points is obtained as input from the user. This implies that each time the density is changed by the user, the whole computation process is done during run time, and this might sometimes crash the application. Hence, to solve this, the UI has an option of clearing the previously generated tetrahedra. This might reduce the overload during run time, and helps avoid crashes, thought not guaranteed.

DT is successfully computed and tested against various other meshes as shown in Figure 5.43. Since, DT is a convex structure, it doesn't work well for a concave structure(see Figure 5.43(a)).

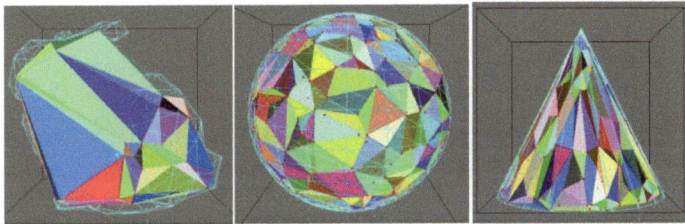

Figure 5.43 (a) DT for a concave structure (b) DT of a sphere with density = 500 (c) DT of a cone with density = 1000

This is allowed depending on the usage of the DT structure. If it is used for fracturing a mesh, this case is acceptable as its dual the voronoi diagrams are needed and not the DT structure in specific (Jose 2011). However, it may not be acceptable in case of mesh generation. Constrained DT is a possible solution to deal with non-convex shapes.

Voronoi diagrams are constructed by joining all the circumcenters of its dual tetrahedra. Edges are formed between two vertices of a Voronoi diagram if and only if the dual of the two vertices are adjacent to each other. Voronoi cells were not generated due to few issues which occurred while programming. Hence, a voronoi skeleton as shown in Figure 5.44 is obtained. The blue points are the voronoi vertices.

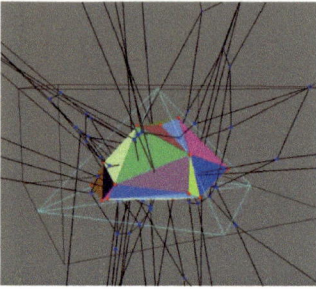

Figure 5.44 Voronoi diagram obtained from its dual DT

Chapter 6

Conclusion

The main task of this thesis is to have a robust implementation of Delaunay Tetrahedralization that takes as input a set of points obtained by sampling a 3D mesh. The techniques used for Sampling is analysed and concluded that SDF provides quick and efficient distribution of points within the volume of a given mesh when compared to Ray intersections.

Furthermore, we implemented Incremental Insertion algorithm as explained by Ledoux (2007) using Flip based algorithm. We presented that, exact arithmetic for evaluating the predicates are mandatory inorder to get a robust, reliable and error-free DT structure. The implementation speed is greatly affected because of it, however it is well handled by adaptive-arithmetic technique proposed by Schewchuck(1997).

6.1 Limitations

For the construction of DT the input mesh has to be convex as the Delaunay cannot recognize interior boundaries and concave faces. It can be solved by using virtual nodes or for non-convex meshes, an extension to DT known as Constrained DT can be used. However, this project only deals with convex meshes. Also, in volume sampling, using ray intersection for points with higher density does not yield satisfactory result as the computations are too heavy and hence the program tend to crash. Hence, for a large dataset of points, the algorithm is not optimised and cannot handle it. Also, DT of datasets that has many degenerate cases could not be constructed as well.

6.2 Future goals

The project was initially started with the idea of Fracturing a 3D Mesh. To do this the mesh has to be fragmented using Voronoi diagrams. Hence, to obtain Voronoi diagrams, Delaunay tetrahedralization was the best way to achieve it, being its dual. This paved way to the idea of this project of computing DT. Having achieved it now, the use of Delaunay tetrahedralization in any application can be looked into. DT's are highly being researched in the area of automatic Mesh Generation.

References

Chew,L,P. 1989. Guaranteed-Quality Triangular Meshes. Technical Report TR-89-983, Department of Computer Science,Cornell University.

Frey, W.H. Selective Refinement: A New Strategy for Automatic Node Placement in Graded Triangular Meshes. International Journal for Numerical Methods in Engineering

Frey,H,W. Selective Refinement: A New Strategy for Automatic Node Placement in Graded Triangular Meshes.International Journal for Numerical Methods in Engineering.

Ledoux, H., 2007. Computing the 3D Voronoi Diagram Robustly:An Easy Explanation.Delft University of Technology [Accessed 28 July 2013].

Jose.2011. Available from : http://www.joesfer.com/?p=84 [Accessed 26 June 2013].

Ruppert,J. 1995. A Delaunay Refinement Algorithm for Quality 2-Dimensional Mesh Generation. Journal of Algorithms 18(3):548–585.

Weatherill,N,P. 1992. Delaunay Triangulation in Computational Fluid Dynamics. Computers and Mathematics with Applications.

Chew,L.,P. Guaranteed-Quality Triangular Meshes. Technical Report TR-89-983, Department of Computer Science.

H.Si, 2004. Tetgen: a quality tetrahedral mesh generator and three-dimensional Delaunay triangulator.

Delone, B. N. Sur la spherevide. Bul. Acad. Sci. URSS, Class. Sci. Nat., 793–800.

Guibas, L. J., and Stolfi, J. 1985. Primitives for the manipulation of general subdivisions and the computation of Voronoi diagrams. ACM Trans. Graphics 4, 74–123.

Fortune, S. 1987. A sweepline algorithm for the Voronoi diagrams. Algorithmica 2, 153–174.

Green,P.,J. and R., Sibson.1977. Computing Dirichlet tesselations in the plane. Computer Journal, 12(2):168–173.

Guibas,L and Stolfi,J. 1985.Primitives for the manipulation of general subdivisions and the computation of Voronoi diagrams. ACM Transactions on Graphics, 4(2):74–123, April.

Joe, B.1989. Three-dimensional triangulations from local transformations. SIAM Journal on Scientific and Statistical Computing, 10(4):718–741.

Guibas,L.,J and Stolfi,J. 1985. Primitives for the Manipulation of General Subdivisions and the Computation of Voronoï Diagrams. ACM Transactions onvGraphics 4(2):74–123, April.

Fortune, S. 1987. A Sweepline Algorithm for Voronoi Diagrams. Algorithmica 2(2):153–17w.

Joe,B.1991. Construction of three-dimensional Delaunay triangulations using local transformations. Computer Aided Geometric Design, 8:123–142.

YOUR KNOWLEDGE HAS VALUE

- We will publish your bachelor's and master's thesis, essays and papers

- Your own eBook and book - sold worldwide in all relevant shops

- Earn money with each sale

Upload your text at www.GRIN.com and publish for free